EXPLORE COLONIAL AMERICA



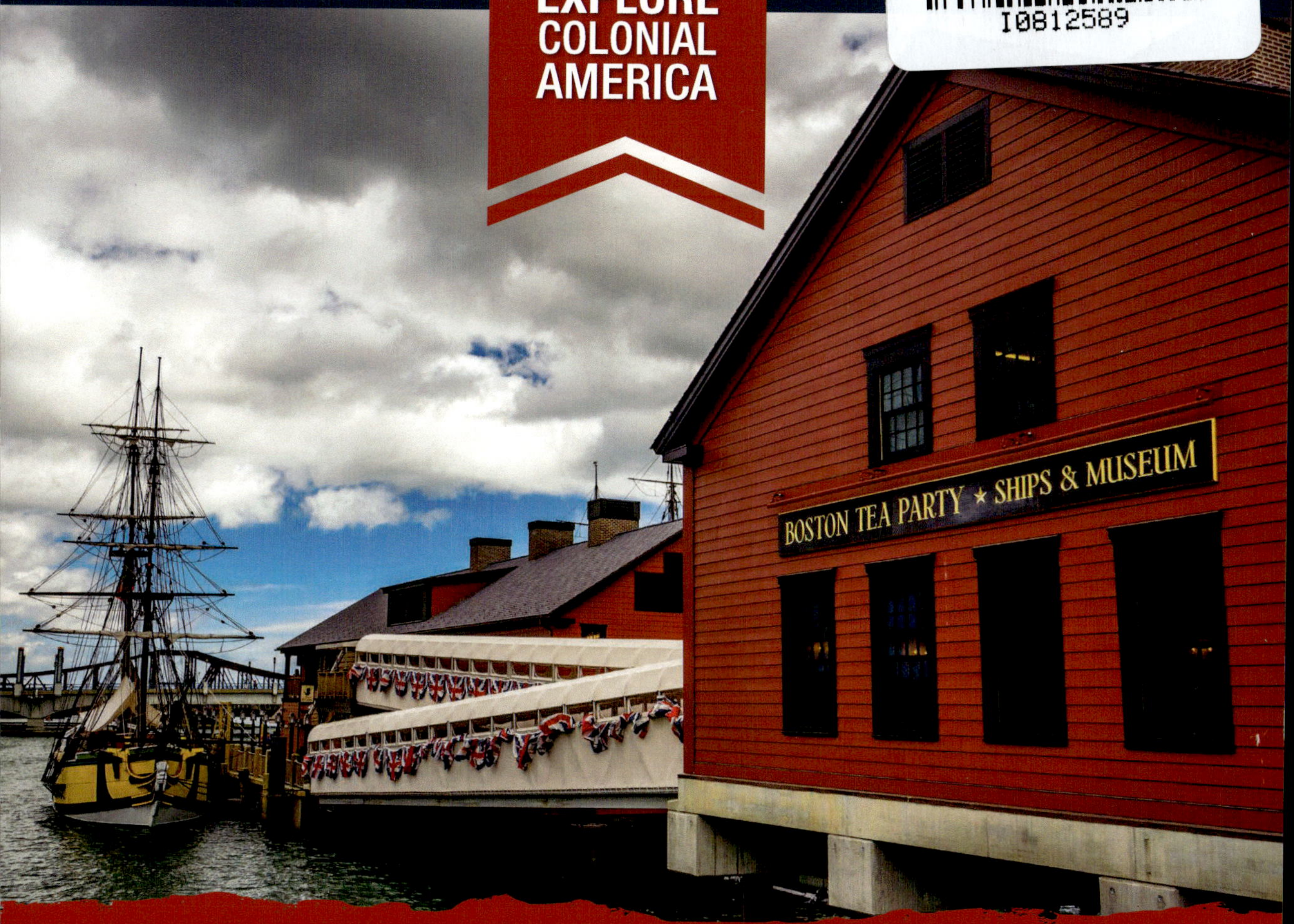


# THE BOSTON TEA PARTY

Sarah Gilman

Enslow Publishing
101 W. 23rd Street
Suite 240
New York, NY 10011
USA
enslow.com

Published in 2017 by Enslow Publishing, LLC.
101 W. 23rd Street, Suite 240, New York, NY 10011



**Library of Congress Cataloging-in-Publication Data**

Names: Gilman, Sarah, author.
Title: The Boston Tea Party / Sarah Gilman.
Description: New York, NY : Enslow Publishing, 2017. | Series: Explore colonial America | Includes bibliographical references and index. | Audience: Ages 9-up. | Audience: Grade 7 to 8.
Identifiers: LCCN 2015050609| ISBN 9780766078727 (library bound) | ISBN 9780766078789 (pbk.) | ISBN 9780766078604 (6-pack)
Subjects: LCSH: Boston Tea Party, Boston, Mass., 1773--Juvenile literature.
Classification: LCC E215.7 .G49 2016 | DDC 973.3/115--dc23
LC record available at http://lccn.loc.gov/2015050609

**To Our Readers:** We have done our best to make sure all website addresses in this book were active and appropriate when we went to press. However, the author and the publisher have no control over and assume no liability for the material available on those websites or on any websites they may link to. Any comments or suggestions can be sent by e-mail to customerservice@enslow.com.

Portions of this book originally appeared in the book *Witness the Boston Tea Party* by Elaine Landau.

**Photo Credits:** Cover, p. 1 John Bilous/Shutterstock.com; p. 4 Public domain/File:Boston, 1775bsmall1.png/Wikimedia Commons; pp. 6, 16, 30 Library of Congress; p. 8 Universal History Archive/Getty Images; pp. 11, 19, 26 Hulton Archive/Getty Images; p. 14 The 'Dartmouth' in Boston Harbour (litho), American School, (19th century) / Private Collection / Peter Newark American Pictures / Bridgeman Images; pp. 20, 32, 33 © North Wind Picture Archives; p. 23 Print Collector/Getty Images; p. 28 Destruction of the tea cargoes, known as the Boston Tea Party, 16 December 1773 (colour litho), American School, (19th century) / Private Collection / Peter Newark American Pictures / Bridgeman Images; p. 35 Public domain/File:Flickr - USCapitol - The First Continental Congress, 1774.jpg/Wikimedia Commons; p. 37 MPI/Getty Images; p. 39 Ed Vebell/Getty Images; p. 40 Stock Montage/Getty Images; p. 43 George F. Mobley/Getty Images.

# CONTENTS

Colonial Boston was the site of many important events. But it was the Boston Tea Party that served as a catalyst to the colonists' independence.

CHAPTER
ONE

# NO TAXATION WITHOUT REPRESENTATION

Trouble had been brewing in the Massachusetts colony for months. The colonists were upset. They felt that they were being treated unfairly and wanted to put a stop to it. They were angry at King George III of Britain and Parliament (the British government). The problem had to do with taxes.

## PUNISHING ACTS

At the time, Britain needed money. It had recently finished fighting a long war against France in both Europe and the colonies. Now it had to pay for the cost of the war. Britain hoped to raise the money by taxing the colonies, who had been helped by the British victory.

Tensions between Britain and its colonists came to a head in the Boston Massacre. This bloody skirmish was a result of the colonists' anger at British soldiers stationed there.

The British Parliament had passed the Tea Act of 1773. This law placed a tax on tea coming into the colonies. Earlier, Parliament had also passed several new taxes on such items as paper, glass, and paint. These taxes were known as the Townsend Acts of 1767. One of these had placed another tax on tea as well. None of this money would be used for the colonists' needs. Instead, the funds would go to Britain.

## EXPLORE THE FACTS

### THE STAMP ACT

The colonists also were upset with the Stamp Act. This act stated that documents, some books, and even playing cards had to be stamped with a special marking that cost money.

The colonists were not about to accept this. They felt that the taxes were not right. The colonists had no elected officials to represent them in the British Parliament. There was no one to stand up for their interests. They argued that there should be "no taxation without representation."

King George III and the British government saw things differently. They said that all British subjects were represented in Parliament. That included those living in the colonies.

This building is believed to be the location where the details of the Boston Tea Party were hatched. This event finally would get Britain's attention.

## A TASTE OF FREEDOM

But the colonists knew that Parliament cared little about them. For years, Britain had largely ignored the colonies. The colonists rarely paid attention to British law and this usually went unpunished. Frequently taxes went uncollected as well.

For the most part, the colonists had been left to govern themselves. They elected their own officials and made their own rules. Living in America had given the colonists a taste of freedom. Now they did not want to be controlled by Britain.

Groups of colonists concerned about the taxes soon formed. They hoped to change things. The Sons of Liberty was one of these groups. There were many others as well. Meetings were held throughout the colonies. Leaders in different colonies wrote to one another. They knew that they had to stay united.

The colonists were determined to be heard. They thought of ways to protest British policies. The British government and their supporters in the colonies saw these individuals as troublemakers and lawbreakers. Yet many colonists saw them as patriots. They were people who loved their new land and were willing to fight for their rights there.

CHAPTER TWO

# BOYCOTT

The colonists wanted Britain to stop taxing their tea. Some tried boycotting (refusing to buy) tea as a form of protest. Colonists had begun to do this earlier because tea was also being taxed under the Townsend Acts of 1767.

Giving up tea had not been easy. Tea was a popular drink in the colonies. It was as popular as soda or chewing gum is today. Can you imagine everyone in the United States giving up these treats? The same would be true for tea in the colonies.

## TEA SUBSTITUTES

The colonists' love of tea made a boycott especially difficult. So they tried to find ways to replace their favorite drink. Many colonial women began brewing herbal teas. They used various plants for different tastes. One popular tea was made from a plant called New Jersey tea, also known as redroot. Grown in swampy areas, redroot has a strong flavor. The local American Indians had drunk it for years.

In this political cartoon, a colonist reads a notice announcing a tax on tea. A British soldier stands guard in the background, holding a rifle and a bayonet. The cartoon's caption notes that the tax "was worse than a bayonet."

The patriots liked the idea of local brews. They encouraged people to drink them. Some colonial doctors helped with this. They claimed that drinking British tea was unhealthy. Some said it would cause nervousness and sickness. Others argued that it could even lead to an early death. Much of this was not true. However, these doctors' claims gave colonists two reasons to boycott tea. They did it because they thought it would improve their health and for the good of the colony.

CHAPTER THREE

# A GREATER THREAT

The boycott hadn't worked exactly. But the colonists' protests of the Townsend Acts had had a positive effect. Britain removed all the taxes except the one on tea. For a time, the colonists felt better. Though the tea boycott continued, it was not strongly followed.

## KEEP THE TEA OUT!

However, the new Tea Act of 1773 again made the colonists furious. It said that the British East India Company could sell its tea in America for half price. This was a threat to American tea traders, who had to sell their tea at regular price. On top of this, the colonists had to pay the usual tax on the British tea. Now the patriots became even more determined than ever.

The colonists attempted to get the *Dartmouth's* to leave Boston Harbor. The ship was loaded with tea, and the colonists believed refusing the cargo would send a message to Britain.

They would keep tea from Britain out of the colonies. All British ships carrying it were to be turned back.

The colonists' determination was soon put to the test. On November 28, 1773, the *Dartmouth* sailed into Boston Harbor. It was the first ship to arrive from Britain with a cargo of tea. The patriots knew that they had to act quickly. First they spoke with the colony's tea merchants. These men worked for the

British East India Company that sent the tea. The patriots asked the merchants to turn the ship around. They wanted the *Dartmouth* to go back to Britain. But the merchants refused. Their loyalty was with Britain. They made their living selling tea.

## EXPLORE THE FACTS

### PATRIOTS

Boston was not the only place where patriots lived. People all over the colonies were angry at the British. In New York, for instance, a barber refused to cut the hair of any British men.

## AN IMPORTANT MEETING

Now the patriots called for a general meeting to see how people felt. On November 29, messengers on horseback were sent out to alert colonists in the surrounding areas. These men rode at top speed. They carried letters urging everyone to come to the meeting the next morning.

By 9:00 a.m. on November 30, a crowd of about five thousand had gathered at Boston's Old South Meeting House. Everyone there was firmly against paying the tea tax. John Hancock, a wealthy Boston merchant and an active patriot, led the meeting. Samuel Adams, another patriot, stressed that the tea must not be allowed to leave the ship. The crowd agreed.

Samuel Adams was an organizer and leader of Boston's radical Sons of Liberty organization. He believed in the power of mob violence to send a message to Britain. It is believed that Adams played a large role in the Boston Tea Party.

The colonists knew that they had to be careful. They did not want to be tricked by the tea merchants. They feared that the merchants might try to secretly unload the tea chests. Once the shipment was on land, the tax had to be paid.

So the patriots had volunteers guard the ship. A force of twenty-five men soon boarded the *Dartmouth*. They carried guns called muskets and worked in shifts. That way the ship was guarded around the clock. The patriots also printed up posters. These warned everyone not to try to unload the ship's cargo. Anyone who did would face an angry mob.

## CHAPTER FOUR

# TENSIONS MOUNT

The colonists' boycott had cost the local tea merchants money. They were very upset, so they went to see the governor of the Massachusetts colony. As the colony's governor, Thomas Hutchinson was an official of the British government. He was also quite disliked by many colonists.

The governor issued a public order to the colony. He demanded that the tea boycott stop. He also wanted no further meetings held. The patriots ignored Hutchinson. They were not about to let him tell them what to do.

## THE LOYALISTS VS. THE PATRIOTS

Yet not everyone in the colony was a patriot. Some were still fiercely loyal to Britain and King George III. These people were called Loyalists or Tories. Tensions between the patriots and the Loyalists grew. The tea merchants became fearful. They did not want to be

Massachusetts governor Thomas Hutchinson was chased by local rioters after demanding a stamp tax from them. His refusal to return the British tea ships to Europe led to the tea party.

harmed or have their property destroyed. Still, at times, violence broke out. A tea merchant named Richard Clarke became a victim of the violence.

The patriots had wanted Clarke to quit his job. That meant he would no longer work as a merchant for the British East India Company. Clarke refused and paid a high price for it. An angry mob damaged his store. Other merchants were threatened, too.

Colonists force a Tory out of town. Patriots could be quite forceful in their beliefs. They damaged merchants' businesses and harmed and humiliated colonists who were loyal to Britain.

# EXPLORE THE FACTS

## TARRING AND FEATHERING

Patriots strong-armed Loyalists and tea merchants who did not agree with them. One of their punishments was to tar and feather those who went along with British Acts.

## COMMUNICATION AMONG THE COLONIES

Through it all, the colonies remained united. Patriots in the cities of New York and Philadelphia followed the lead of those in Boston. No ships carrying tea from England entered their ports. In Philadelphia, all the tea merchants resigned. Those in the New York colony did the same.

Despite the distance between the different colonies, the patriots stayed in close touch. Messengers rode back and forth bringing news. They galloped through rainstorms and sleet. Sometimes they were on the road for days. But they knew they had an important job to do.

Patriots in Philadelphia and New York cheered on the Boston colonists. They urged them to stay strong. The patriots in Boston would need both strength and courage. On December 7, two more British ships arrived in port. Both carried tea shipments. These were the *Eleanor* and the *Beaver*. Soon, the patriots would have to make a very hard decision: What should they do about all these British tea ships?

## CHAPTER FIVE

# NO OTHER CHOICE

They patriots found themselves in a difficult position. British law called for a tax on any tea brought into the harbor by ship. December 16 was the last day before the tax was due.

## TIME IS RUNNING OUT

If the colonists did not act, the tea owners would pay the tax. Then, British customs officers would take the tea off the ships. They would use force if necessary. After that, the tea merchants would sell the tea. They would charge their customers tax to make up for the tax they paid Britain.

The patriots knew that not all the colonists supported the boycott. Some were still loyal to Britain. Others just wanted a good cup of tea. They were willing to pay the British tax.

The patriots did not have very much time left. They had to come up with an answer quickly. A meeting was called for December 16.

That day, colonists poured into Boston. They could be seen coming for miles. The large number of people could not even fit into the Old South Meeting House.

Furious colonists gathered to read copies of the Stamp Act. Although not all colonists were in favor of taking a stand against Britain, a small but powerful group was ready to act.

## ANOTHER REFUSAL

The patriots had asked a man named Francis Rotch to be there. He was the son of the *Dartmouth*'s owner. The elder Rotch had been asked to send his ship back to Britain. However, the British customs officers would not allow the ship to leave until the tax was paid.

The colonists at the meeting sent Francis Rotch to see Governor Hutchinson. He asked the governor if his father's ship could set sail. The governor refused. Also, the British Royal Navy warships *Active* and *Kingfisher* were under orders to prevent any tea ships from leaving without permission.

At that point, the patriots faced a tough decision. For weeks, some of them had met in secret. They discussed throwing the tea overboard. However, they tried to avoid breaking the law. Now, they felt that they had few choices left. That night they would turn Boston's harbor into one big teapot.

CHAPTER SIX

# A NIGHT OF DESTRUCTION

Even if they felt they had no other choice, the decision was a hard one. The patriots were putting themselves at great risk. British warships were anchored in the waters close by. If the British caught the patriots, things would not go well for them. They could be arrested. Some might even be shot on the spot.

Therefore, secrecy was especially important that night. After dark, the men went to their secret meeting places. There, they hurriedly tried to disguise themselves.

## READY TO TAKE A STAND

The men dressed like Mohawk Indians. They wrapped blankets around their shoulders and tied feathers in their hair. They carried tomahawks (axes) and clubs.

The patriots disguised themselves as Mohawks before they committed their acts. This signaled that they considered themselves American, not subjects of Britain.

Then they headed for Griffin's Wharf. That is where the ships carrying the tea were docked. The patriots arrived in small groups. Some were very young, like fourteen-year-old Peter Slater.

Most of the men had gone down Milk Street and then on to Hutchinson Street. People heard them coming and ran to their windows. They felt that something important was about to happen. They were right.

## DESTROYING THE TEA

As the men assembled on Griffin's Wharf, they quickly divided into three groups. Each had a leader who had been picked beforehand. There were about 150 patriots in all.

There was no time to lose. Carrying lanterns and torches, the men boarded the ships. They were prepared to take the vessels by force. But as it turned out, that was not necessary. The British crews did not resist.

Once on board, the men opened the hatches. They soon found what they were looking for. The cargo area was filled with chests of tea.

Each chest weighed about three hundred pounds. The men pulled the heavy wooden chests up to the deck. It was tiring work and their arms ached. Yet no one stopped to rest. Fifteen-year-old Joshua Wyeth would later say, "I never worked harder in my life."

The patriots split the tea chests open with their tomahawks. Then they heaved the tea into the water. The men smashed the empty chests, too. They threw the wood pieces overboard as well.

After boarding the British ships, the patriots opened the cargo and dumped the tea into Boston Harbor. This act of defiance would shock the British Parliament and force the king to take the colonists seriously.

# EXPLORE THE FACTS

## A RALLYING SONG

The day after the tea party, a song was created. It began with the lines, "Rally, Mohawks! Bring out your axes, And tell King George we'll pay no taxes."

The clang of the Mohawks' tomahawks rang out in the night. The sound drew a crowd to the wharf. Over a thousand people left their homes to see what was going on.

## THE DEED IS DONE

It took about three hours to finish the job. In all, 342 chests of tea were ruined. No other damage was done to the ship.

This was very important to the men. They saw themselves as patriots, not criminals. They had only come to destroy the tea. The crew and other cargo were not touched. Before going, they even swept the decks clean.

On the way home, some of the patriots passed a house where a British admiral was visiting. He had seen everything from the window. When the admiral heard the "Mohawks" outside, he called out to them. (The British knew the Mohawks were really colonists.) He told the men that they would pay for what they had done. It was their first warning of things to come.

Other colonists cheered on the patriots as they destroyed the British cargo. They enjoyed this evening of triumph before waiting for Britain's response.

The patriots knew that the British would be angry, but they did not know just how important their tea party was. After that night the colonies would never be the same. How would the British show their anger? Should the colonists be preparing for war? Only the coming months would give the colonists the answers they needed.

## CHAPTER SEVEN

# THE REACTION TO THE TEA PARTY

It didn't take long for news of the patriots' activities to spread. Colonists in New York and Philadelphia admired the Boston patriots' bravery. People in other colonies felt the same way. As it turned out, the Boston colonists had set an example. Soon there were other tea parties in different colonies.

## PAYING THE PRICE

King George III and Parliament were not happy. They were determined to punish the Boston colonists. To do so, Parliament passed the Boston Port Act. As of June 1, 1774, Boston Harbor was closed. No ships could go in or out until the destroyed tea was paid for.

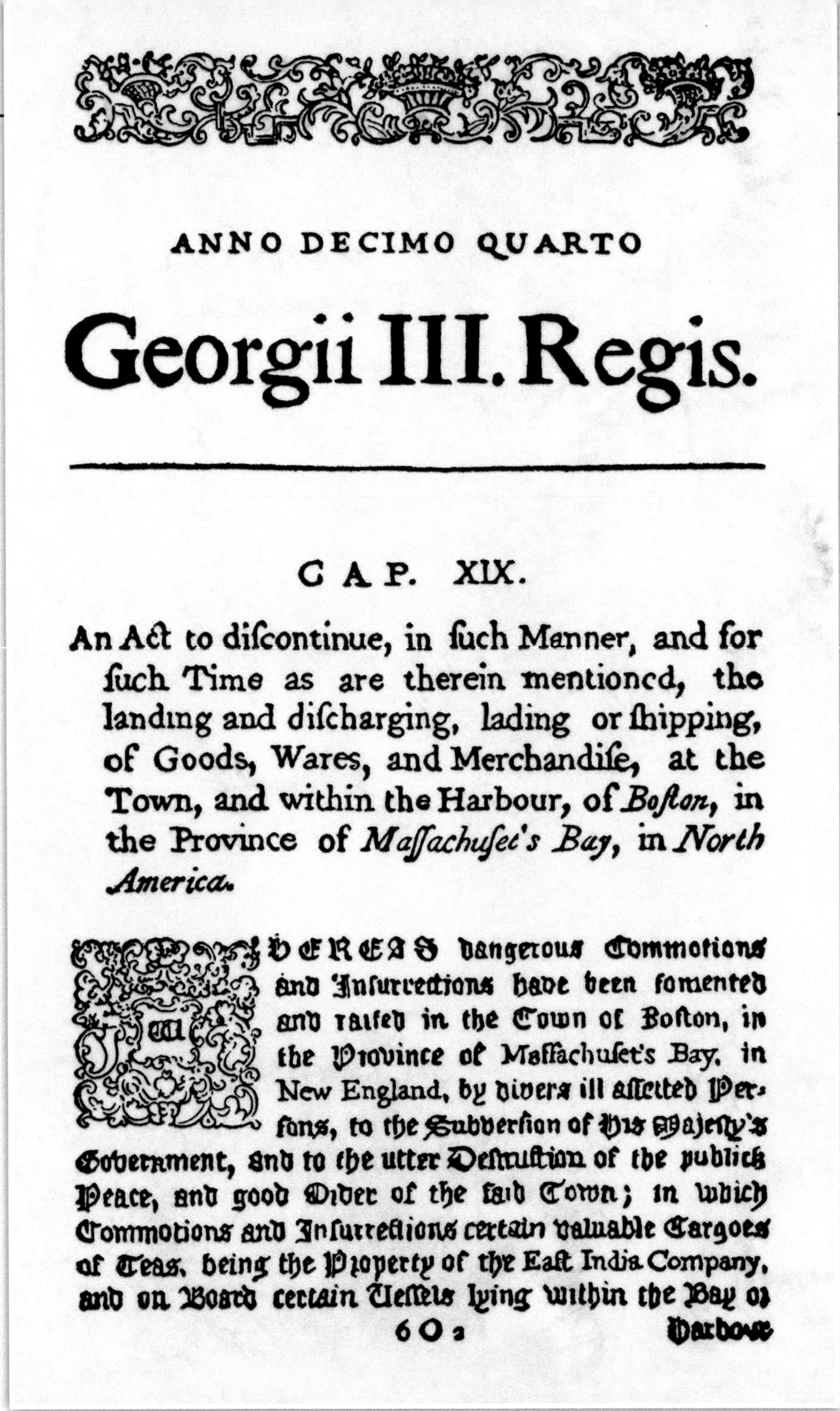

ANNO DECIMO QUARTO

# Georgii III. Regis.

CAP. XIX.

An Act to discontinue, in such Manner, and for such Time as are therein mentioned, the landing and discharging, lading or shipping, of Goods, Wares, and Merchandise, at the Town, and within the Harbour, of *Boston*, in the Province of *Massachuset's Bay*, in *North America*.

WHEREAS dangerous Commotions and Insurrections have been fomented and raised in the Town of Boston, in the Province of Massachuset's Bay, in New England, by divers ill affected Persons, to the Subversion of His Majesty's Government, and to the utter Destruction of the publick Peace, and good Order of the said Town; in which Commotions and Insurrections certain valuable Cargoes of Teas, being the Property of the East India Company, and on Board certain Vessels lying within the Bay or

60 2 Harbour

King George reacted very badly to the Boston Tea Party. Parliament passed the Boston Port Act, one of several "Intolerable Acts" meant to show the colonists who was boss.

This hurt the Massachusetts colonists. Many of them made their living through shipping. Nevertheless, the colonists voted against paying for the ruined tea.

Britain was not about to give up either. Still more laws were passed to limit the Massachusetts colonists' freedom. Now these colonists could no longer elect their own officials. Britain

To punish the colonists further, Parliament passed the Quartering Act. The law allowed British soldiers to take over any place they wished in Boston. This included colonists' homes.

Realizing they needed to band together, the colonies sent representatives to Philadelphia for the First Continental Congress.

appointed them instead. Public meetings were outlawed, too. A law called the Quartering Act was especially hard on the colonists. According to this act, British soldiers could be sheltered anywhere their officers chose. This included the colonists' homes.

Many of the colonists in Massachusetts were angry. They even called these unfair laws the Intolerable Acts. This meant that the colonists mostly found these laws impossible to accept.

## THE FIRST CONTINENTAL CONGRESS

Leaders in other colonies grew angry as well. They saw what Britain was doing to the Massachusetts colonists. They wondered if their colony would be next.

They decided to meet in Philadelphia in September 1774. This gathering became known as the First Continental Congress. All the colonies sent men to represent them except Georgia. However, this southern colony agreed in advance to any decisions the Congress made.

Through the First Continental Congress, the colonists let Britain know where they stood. The colonists refused to obey unfair laws. They would not pay unfair taxes either. The Congress also called for a boycott of British goods.

The colonists did not know what King George III and Parliament would do next. But they feared the worst. They knew that Britain might use its army against them. If that happened, the colonists were ready to fight back. They felt that the freedom and liberty they were used to were now at stake.

CHAPTER EIGHT

# THE SHOT HEARD ROUND THE WORLD

There wasn't much time to act. The colonists needed to put together an army quickly. Most of these men had never been soldiers before. They were farmers, laborers, and merchants. Many were teenagers. A few were grandfathers.

## THE MINUTEMEN

Now, after a full day's work, they did military drills. In Massachusetts, the men formed militias. They called themselves Minutemen. They were ready and willing to fight on a minute's notice.

The colonists desperately needed weapons as well. They soon collected every available musket and a good supply of gunpowder. They stored these in Concord—a town near Boston.

The colonies needed to assemble a militia quickly in order to defend themselves against Britain. The Minutemen gathered whatever guns and ammunition they could find.

The British were also prepared to fight. British General Thomas Gage was the new governor of the Massachusetts colony. Gage had spies working for him. They told him about the colonists' stored weapons at Concord. He also learned that Samuel Adams and John Hancock were hiding in Lexington—just miles from Concord. These men had become very important patriot leaders. Gage hoped to catch them.

## THE MIDNIGHT RIDE

In April 1775, Gage made his move. He sent seven hundred soldiers to Lexington to arrest Adams and Hancock. From there, the soldiers were to go on to Concord to seize the weapons. The British did not think highly of the colonists' poorly trained militias. They felt certain of success.

However, the patriots had their own spies. They learned about Gage's plan. Then the colonists sprang into action.

Gage's soldiers were to reach Lexington on April 19. But on the night of April 18, a patriot named Paul Revere made his famous midnight ride. He rode through the countryside at top speed, warning the colonists that the British were coming. Paul Revere reached Samuel Adams and John Hancock before Gage's soldiers did. The pair escaped in time.

## BATTLE OF LEXINGTON AND CONCORD

When the British arrived in Lexington, the Minutemen were waiting for them. Gage's soldiers far outnumbered the patriots. But the Minutemen were not about to run and hide. They bravely faced their enemy.

Shots rang out. No one is sure which side fired first. However, before it was over, eight Minutemen were dead. About ten more were wounded.

From Lexington, the British troops went on to Concord. Fighting broke out there as well. Both sides lost men.

Luckily, the British were unable to complete their mission. Most of the weapons hidden at Concord had already been moved. The British were only able to destroy a small part of the colonists' supply.

**Paul Revere embarked on a famous midnight ride to warn colonists that the British army was approaching. From this point, events happened very quickly.**

# EXPLORE THE FACTS

## TWO MIDNIGHT RIDES?

Paul Revere was not the only one who tried to warn people of the approaching British. William Dawes, a Boston tanner, also rode his horse to raise the alarm.

Minutemen were put to the test quickly, when the shot heard round the world was fired. Battles at Lexington and Concord kicked off the Revolutionary War.

## ON TO BOSTON

Then the British began their march back to Boston. At that point, they thought the fighting was over. They did not count on what happened next.

Though the British thought they were alone, they were not. The Minutemen had been quietly trailing them. Suddenly, the British soldiers heard shots. The Minutemen had begun firing at them from behind trees, barns, and fences.

The British could not see their enemy. They did not know where the bullets were coming from. Hopelessly, they tried to fire back. But the Minutemen had the upper hand. By the time they reached Boston, the British had lost about two hundred fifty men.

The fighting at Lexington and Concord changed life in the colonies forever. The famous poet Ralph Waldo Emerson later wrote about that day. He described the patriots as firing "the shot heard round the world." These battles marked the start of a long and difficult war. The American Revolution had begun.

CHAPTER NINE

# THE TEA PARTY'S LEGACY

If the patriots had never tossed that tea overboard, America might be a very different place today. The Boston Tea Party was one of the nation's most important events. It proved to be much more than just an act of protest. Britain's harsh reaction to it caused the colonists to unite. They saw how much freedom meant to them. They were willing to fight and die for it.

When the American Revolution was over, the colonies were an independent nation. In time, that nation grew into one of the world's most powerful countries—the United States of America. Yet it all began with the Boston Tea Party.

## AN ICONIC EVENT

Today, people still celebrate the Boston Tea Party by tossing fake chests of tea into Boston Harbor. The act of resistance and

The Boston Tea Party is such a significant event in American history that people come to Boston every year to reenact the dumping of tea overboard into the harbor.

rebellion is considered a symbol of American freedom. People still refer to it today during times of political protest.

Of course, the colonists taking part in the real Boston Tea Party never imagined its importance. They were simply demanding fair treatment. It just shows what can happen when people stand up for what they believe in.

# TIMELINE

**1767**

The Townsend Acts are passed taxing a number of household items used by the colonists.

**1773**

**November 28**—The *Dartmouth* sails into Boston Harbor.

**November 29**—Messengers leave the Boston colony to call for a general meeting.

**November 30**—Meeting held in Boston with over five thousand colonists attending.

**December 7**—The *Eleanor* and the *Beaver* arrive in Boston—both ships are carrying tea shipments.

**December 16 (day)**—Meeting held in Boston; Francis Rotch speaks to the group; **(evening)**—The Boston Tea Party takes place.

**1774**

**June 1**—The British close Boston Harbor.

**September**—The First Continental Congress is held.

**1775**

**April 18**—Paul Revere makes his famous midnight ride.

**April 19**—The battles at Lexington and Concord are fought.

**1793**

**October 8**—John Hancock dies.

**1803**

**October 2**—Samuel Adams dies.

**1818**

**May 10**—Paul Revere dies.

# GLOSSARY

**BOYCOTT**—To refuse to buy something.

**CARGO**—Goods carried by a ship.

**COLONY**—A group of people who settle in a new land.

**LOYALIST**—A person who was loyal to Britain.

**MERCHANT**—Someone who sells goods.

**MILITIA**—A group of citizens trained to fight in an emergency.

**MUSKET**—A type of gun used before there were rifles.

**PARLIAMENT**—A form of government in Britain in which people are elected to office. They pass laws to govern the nation.

**PATRIOT**—A person who loves his or her country.

**PROTEST**—A public demonstration expressing dissapproval for something.

**TAXATION**—Money that must be paid by people to support their government.

**VOLUNTEER**—Offering to do a job or task without pay.

**WHARF**—A dock where boats can load and unload.

# FURTHER READING

Brennan, Linda Crotta. *The Boston Tea Party.* Ann Arbor, MI: Cherry Lake Publishing, 2013.

Crompton, Samuel Etinde. *The Boston Tea Party: Colonists Protest the British Government.* New York: Chelsea House, 2011.

Cunningham, Kevin. *The Boston Tea Party.* Danbury, CT: Children's Press, 2013.

Gondosch, Linda. *How Did Tea and Taxes Spark a Revolution? And Other Questions About the Boston Tea Party.* Minneapolis: Lerner Publications, 2011.

Jeffrey, Gary and Nick Spender. *Samuel Adams and the Boston Tea Party.* New York: Gareth Stevens Publishing, 2012.

Krull, Kathleen and Lauren Mortimer. *What Was the Boston Tea Party?* New York: Grosset & Dunlap, 2013.

Malaspina, Ann. *The Boston Tea Party.* Minneapolis: ABDO Publishing Company, 2013.

Perritano, John. *The Causes of the American Revolution.* New York: Crabtree Publishing Company, 2013.

# FOR MORE INFORMATION

## THE BOSTON TEA PARTY SHIP & MUSEUM

**www.bostonteapartyship.com**

Visit the site of the museum that recreates the Boston Tea Party for visitors. Don't miss the replicas of the ships.

## THE AMERICAN REVOLUTION

**www.nps.gov/revwar/about_the_revolution/timeline_of_events_06_10.html**

Check out this website from the National Park Service to learn about the events of the American Revolution.

## THE PAUL REVERE HOUSE

**www.paulreverehouse.org**

This site tells everything you'd want to know about the famous patriot Paul Revere.

# INDEX